Days of Earthly Exile

Also by Alexandra Sashe

Antibodies
Convalescence Dance

Alexandra Sashe

Days of Earthly Exile

Shearsman Books

First published in the United Kingdom in 2021 by
Shearsman Books
PO Box 4239
Swindon
SN3 9FN

Shearsman Books Ltd Registered Office
30–31 St. James Place, Mangotsfield, Bristol BS16 9JB
(this address not for correspondence)

www.shearsman.com

ISBN 978-1-84861-771-1

Contents

Part I

Part 2

*"By the rivers of Babylon,
there we sat down, yea, we wept…"*
(Ps. 137:1)

Part 1

On the left shore of the pain
we dance
    light as feathers.

We collect the discordant movements,
a thousand threads
      from the bandages
of our bleached sleeveless
days.

The solitary voice of the pain
breaks through the birds' voice,
the rooms' silence, the dry
sound of marbles.

    The sand of the shore
    swallows
    our dance, whiteness and pain.

At the harbour we dance
upon the ropes
along the tight Gordian moorings:

Our eyes are swimmers, and –
    the oars of our memory
    make no splash,
  and the boat
    leaves no wake.

On the left shore of the pain
we are beginners, apprentices
of the simple coherent movements.
                              We dip the edge
of the words we spared
into white paint.

                    Our dance is a still
                    whitewashed
                              and effaced
                    landscape.

What we hear of our aching harmony
is the nudity of the Garden.
We lay together the spared words
to compose
our common name, –

                    we sow the omission points,
                    plant flowers
                    for hyphens.

    (Moored on the right shore, the pain
                              is our vessel. –
    We unfurl the wind for a sail.)

Autumnal

As the sun put locks upon our treasure
and the autumn time dried and clothed
our hands with stillness,
                    As the hay is burnt for hunger, –
We throw our heads backwards and gently observe
the birds resting upon their wings in flight.

Copper and fire yield
to our alms-begging songs : we collect their warmth and colour.
A lit candle is our guest and host,
is our home. –
            We are
    its sole
    treasure and light.

We sow in the Land the cries
of birds we don't follow –

we were chosen by Autumn to stay
and till with your eyes the sky.

We gather sun and shade
in barns
and in the damp air leave

imprints of our breath,
of our slow step,
as we wind the fields' clocks
with our faithful unflying hands.

The trees kneel and embrace the fog
and bury roots deeper in sleep;
they were chosen by Autumn to give :
fruits for a fall, leaves for a wing.

We remain immobile among the days,
amongst the space of withered grass,
we learn from the trees to bury and yield,
to fly in sleep,
        to kneel and embrace.

What we join
is poignant   half-true   circumscribed
within the myopic and windy
circles
we dare to draw upon the sand

We silence the speech of our mouth
with cherries and knowledge. And dare to draw
in joined circles
our names
upon the sand.

What we convert into sleep
and augurs
the nimble passage of our hands
retracing the circles
upon the sand
is faithful   is standing
                    is ever-elided.

We call upon that
         whereof we bear
and dare not speak
the name
with our mouth of fault and wonder.

   What we plant in the ground
   and search in the air is
   lachrymal   constant   righteous   wounded,
   the cuts and remnants
   of time circles

wherein we are buried
in sand.

via the candle's growing
down towards its purpose, via the snow
melting its heart.
   via the wedded
wax and thaw water.

It is the last notes of the Song, carrying bread
to the mouth of fullness. It is our praise,
the embrace of our
frailty, love, duty. It is our
Song of the sole recourse.

And the Spring replaces us, stitch by stitch.
Our eyes are carried away beyond the sun.
In the puddles, strangers search
for the reflections of our wings, –

it is our last Song,
once we have outlived the last.

I am given a boat, a sail and an island –

a firm ground of sand,
the days returning, the knot
of water and skies
   at the far end of my sight.

   I am given a windowsill
   and a landscape
   and eyes to follow the birds' flight.

I am given sense of the fullness of hunger,
a perfect repletion of other senses,
a deeper sense of living a still-life,
of baking bread
         from daily breadcrumbs.

      I am given a wing and a thin, transparent
      unbreakable thread, tied to the perch.

I am given myself as precious ballast
to be shed piece by piece –
from the *my* to the *self*.

When the wind breathes you in
your shadow departs, loosed from obedience
free from guilt.   The sun scourges around you:
                                        circles of Whiteness.

                    A blind afternoon gropes about
                    the holes and crevices
                    in the shutters, the tares of solstice
                    are sown among
                    the insomniac seeds of somnolence.

Nothing marine or fluvial
for the sake of this arid de-rivered country.

The hourglass imprisons
the sand of ever-divided shores.
The sundial denies:
        circles of Surface.

From zenith to zenith
we pace the dwelling
of our circular land-locked wharfs,
    and tell the years
    counter-clockwise
    upon the beads of our sand.

It is time to replace
units of time
with units of being-without-act,
with a tree growing down towards its shadow,
with the shadow describing its ultimate circle.

At the edge of the white blossoming field,
it is time to harvest the absence of hunger,
to develop transparent unfoldable wings,

to renounce walking, deny space, –
and collect its smallest
unbreakable fragments.

With the nascent melody of the silence,
with its intervals and the dying
echoes of steps and voices,
it is time –

to count the gold of denials,
to exit time
through its instant-long
                corridors.

If I put my arm around my shoulder
and take my hand
and invite me to dance,

my soul will envelop
my body,
          embrace it
and close the circuit.

          I will enter
          an open space,
                    the static hidden between movements:
          in our dance, the shape of my body
          will merge with the silhouette of my soul,

                    and I coincide with their pas,
                    and am a pirouette
                    and a soundless kingdom.

We will dance knee-level above the ground,
breathe sunlight, minutes and diamonds.

   A shaft of light
   sister and bride of the cupola
   will dissolve my eyes and give me
                              sight.

Land(e)escapes

The further pearls of this arid space
the fissured days.
      and we jump from the cliffs,
      our hands are wounded
      with sea.

We can swim ourselves across the summer.
Our dreams are
and remain unharmed
by the mollified glass-splinters.

The sleep has lost our part.
The thirst has quenched the open eyes
  with salt and safe distances, with ourselves,
  with sea creatures.

Our lungs are drunk to the bottom
by the wind that uncovers us
to the sand.

This lake is a secret impossibility
a one-shore soleness
cognate to eye.

A plexus of focal distances
that justifies its surface.

Bells wash their evening sounds.
Echoes sink, and the carillon gives
each one apiece
a viatical blessing.

The disburdened birds return to the lake
– the tree is their crown and sister – and
they believe in its waters.

They know of an unattainable height
of the eyes that dwell
above the tower.

At dawn they weave
from leaves and feathers
a nest
pure of purpose and calling. –
With every strike of the morning bell
they deny
themselves
above the lake surface.

We are at the edge of time, you see,
in this quieted open space.
   The river is green and endless.

   Hours' beads, unseen and sewn
by strange eyes, with our hands
along its hem.

Breadcrumbs devout to stillness, to our palms
full of air,
            of sacrificial white silence.

   The wood is our chosen embrace.
   And steps are small and endless and river-green.

This slow mountain
breathes us in and out
and holds us safe
            within its lungs.

A day passage, walked and espoused,
becomes an oath,
becomes a path.

The walls awaiting the ruins are home,
home and promise.

A honeysuckle, a syllable:
the winter is named,
named and abolished.

The small, the hidden, the bluebell words
of the Fatherland, written
in harsh, in milk
upon the skin, the veins, the stencil lines
of my palms.

I have ploughed the thought of the Land,
have brought
the rugged, the furrowed, to a white
a smooth, a clean
paper.

                    I have washed the sky
                    and erased the night
from my sleep, my sleepless, my walk
to the temple.

I have learnt a motionless time, –
and drink
from the sole unsinkable
confident flight
of a morning owl.

With a quiet step Spring transcends
its thaw, – with an amorous hand
breaks the mirrors.
    Its ardour leaves unstirred the surface
    of spring water, smooth the surface
    made of cloth, of virgin paper,
    of stained porcelain.

The Spring justifies him who receives it
with cupped hands,
with open arms,
with naked face
and uncovered shoulders;
with palm branches
  and mute mute
    solitary walks
up and down the hill.

St. Veronica's hands

Face imprint,
          forerunner
of the indelible presence.
St. Veronica's hands
nurse your heart to display its chambers
with lace curtains and wooden benches
with light as a banner, and bread
filling your cupped hands as baskets.

The Face remains
          with eyes closed
lighting your passages through the eyelids
breaking the winds and winding the clocks,
substituting Its eyes for their mechanisms.

Bare feet embrace the distance
between the passages of your chambers,
embrace the desert and humid months.
Your lighthouses are
          milestones
extinguished and scattered
to pave the courtyard.
          To the words that called you
          without an echo
          the Face contains your words of response.

Silver threads of water
and silent bells
of an accomplished *say*
delivered from its cords.

The distune is no longer a pending lampshade,
pending hours, awaiting's pendants.

The *say* paces the crystal distance
between
the sunlight and sun-abyss. It evens out
in its bound hands
the weight of the bridges and broken bridges.

The content blended with its form
sheds the filling,
the stitches, the needles :
the verbal knots dissolve their purpose
beyond the bound freedom of meaning.

the north-west-ward gusts of the Leste
recognise their silhouettes at my window,
they read the comfort
of the precious patches of sunlight,
traces of dim revelations
kept safely in retrospection
    of the upholstery of the armchair.

they read consolation of the exact figures
the sunlight imprints with its apparitions
in our morning-orbited being, in our afternoon
passing, sun-minded,
        from room to room.

they come to quench their thirst
for twins, siblings, resemblance;
the windowpane offers a window reflection,
      a naked sill, an Achilles' point.

the gusts collect in their entwined hands
the fragments of faces that saw them off, –

they weave wreaths
      to crown the vanquished
hour of the solstice.

They desert at the equinox and return
to settle and weave nests
  on our sill

in our voices
in our woollen sun-minded being,

on the keyboard they play
anathema
            to the Leste,
the boomerang wind
        going from South to South.

from Confessions

When the rail-ends shuttle
your Past ripens,
  the months are a handful
of snow and foliage;
your burnt offering is a city –
the ashes thereof,
    a fallow soil.

A given land, a home of promise.
Schauflergasse, shepherd of stillness, –
     your season of coming
to kneel to water.
Cobbleseeds sown, and yield in the harvest
elision vowels of your silence.

A birth from the burial of the Past, –
   in the renatal chamber
   of ab-
    solution.

We return to the element –
　　　we bypass the rain. The raw skin of the earth
we walk, kneading into it
our surface.

On our soles we bring home
the damp foliage, the silent jubel.

　　　We can both,
　　　　　light a candle and read the soles:
our lifelines perfected by leaves'
humble bloodless
　　reticulations.

Fire has never known a home,
nor circles. Its birth
ever-pure -raw   -virgin.

　　　We read its naked letters
　　　and let them melt
　　　upon its tongue.

We whisper away our humid hands,
　　　and burn the envelopes. Flames' crown
　　　leaves no traces, no names, no ashes.

　　　　　We never drown.

Our home is
a dry well. Our home
is a ladder
        of one
sole mount.

the last homage to P. Celan

From the letter, inanimate
– my orphan, his anima –
half-path between
grass and hay:
half-feathered, half-weathered
half-buried and half-winged

a lapis lazuli opens the space,
    the king of his own letter
bequeaths his language: his pain and
his secret –
    a portion of each
    he takes

    into the river.

The Square is freed from the name of the tree
it served not, –
and keeps its leaf
  dry and hidden
among the pages that speak of the king:

who speaks
  through his thirst
his hunger.

Our
hands navigate through the river.
Our breaths live.

The hour stands full of earth
and truth. It stands.
It sings its vicinity

to the sun.
                    The oblique rays are faithful
                                        to their path.
                    The air embraces and keeps
                    knowledge of our footsteps.

We call the day by its maiden name:
she stands, earthful
and truthful. She stands.
Her song is a hymn to her white dress.

                    Its hem is our
                        white habit.

This Land, an hourglass that stands
the flow of the sand :
a Landstand
        from earth to heaven
        down- and up-
                rooted.

                    Its song full of birds
                    nesting on earth is their hymn
                                        to the blessing of poverty :
                    to the trees who forsook their roots –

                        who come and
                        inherit the earth.

Our silent hands are found
good and eager
to make a path

secret and trodden
and loyal
to those
who walk away
from path-knowing:

bare and unassuming feet
counselled by the grass.

Our eyes see and confess
how bottomless are the hollows
of our hands,
  how sky-blue.
              How clear and warm
is the second water
wherein we dip a milky cloth,

threads unwoven
from our naked
              barren
          denied
      memory.

From the cloven words
of our common poem,
our cleft
    mutually
    being non-being

our split cords and
double-edged ploughs
over the earth that travels north.

From every letter where we elide
shadow-ways,
                southwards
from the written

from our daily self-denials
and coming
to stand
in the mid-point.

We walk across
our weathered
demi-seasonal rope bridges

        our rootless grass, shallow soil,
        flooded countries

where we own
our water,
own the crust, its bread and its given.

Where we gather
a handful of milestones

and loose the earth,
  South-ridden.

When the day offers a key and a blossom,
a stay for yesterday's wounded shoot,
a clean page and a white porcelain, – an arm

to lean upon and to guide
in and out
the hourcircles.

When the birds are no longer crows,
no longer audible, seen and stranded, –
and the name of the park is replaced
with the name of the Garden,

and the right hand
ploughs and sows,
and the left is safe
in its unknowing.

The tree bearing nests for fruits
offers us home, to bear with us.

When we are ripe and fall on the ground –
    the day will offers us:
    a key and a blossom.

Part 2

Pastoral

The steeple subsists, imbedded
in its future,
its foveal round-about sight
blesses the birds, the inflammable hay,
pilgrims' vicarious nests.

Hungry and even steps and hands
laid on the ground before the porch.
The shade of the Song on the eyes, and walls
of the sun, all sun.

The evening falls
          with mercy and psalms,
with spinning threads
of forbearance.

The rays on the wounded living hands
are baking the last
          morning bread.

Pastoral

Via the Land, via the hours'
fluid awaiting texture,
their unshared and common pace
woven by clocks, by the embracing landscape

Of the home changing its face
via the sun's wrinkles, fields' furrows,
    aging towards its birth

the Song of the tongue resting upon
the objects' silence, muteness, withdrawal, –
    the sole verse of a single word
            sings for
          and out of Love

The wise hands are falling apart,
they sing their fall, and take rest in hay.

The hour touches the land and fills to the brim the cups
of those who were called the last, and came.

Yet the birds' flight
lilac and rose,
                mute and forbidden,
is encountered and received
in the hands
whose embers

are beads of the evening rosary,
whose burns are read in secret
by a child knowing
their fortune.

Patient fingers unfold
their even layers
                of birdly purpose.
        Grains of corn are laid
        for gold, in hands
        that carry the sun.

Fields' mouth, clothed with obedience,
partakes of the clouds' embrace
and blessing.

It is grass, ever-white with her maiden name,
that belongs to her bridegroom, and
waits at the gate.

On the top of the hill
there are white silent petals,
the scent of breast milk,
  the flowers of
          humility.

On the top of the hill there are white and silent
animals: monospecies,
the last unicorn's cousins – extinct,
and thousand-times
              removed.

On the top of the hill
grow benevolent stones
soft and yearning
to cushion the blessed
time-and-again fair and wreathed
heads.

There are Lenten hands
on the top of the hill
kneading
white clay
weaving palm leaves:
jars and baskets
empty of memories

At the foot of the hill there are
clouds and steps,
and the birds of the air

sleeping in grass –
who embrace the invisible roots of the tree
growing its fruits :
the cross and the ladder.

A vernal sun occupies my place,
a solitary demi-seasonal
mezzo-soprano whisper.

Elided vowels make their way back
at a quiet pace.

The plane tree will shed in retrospect
over the square
abandoned and disavowed property of
the ante-renatal words:

husks and petals
in heartfuls   in handfuls.

With a morning step
I come to the door
to the door-stead, the nebulous,
the commencement.

The South is open, and stands
 at the far side of the space.

The silent language that lives by signs
dwells in the mid-throat,
sings
  praises.

The open chest of the Garden
encases its virgin *Prunus padus*, –

  my song dips its hem
   into the nebulous white paint.

I share the bandages from my temples
with the wounded clock, with the window
that stands upright.

With a morning step, I come to the sill
to the forelight, the vitreous:
                      the commencement.

I exchange with the clock
my face and time
and cede to the sun
all mirrors.

for St. Theresa of Lisieux

Offer the Lord
   the hold of your breath,
   a high-pitched silence,
   unknowable days'
         razor-sharp equilibrium. –

(the sublimation of tissue will offer itself).

      The life-long union
          of lungs and oxygen
     dissolves into unity,
        breath by breath.

Flowers close their petals
over the secret, the month, the flavour
of common dwelling;

the crossing of fields
retains the steps,
the footprints, the vanishing point,
the vantage
of the
   eternalised walker.

With the evening eye
    we place our faults
under the window's opaque
magnifying glass :

we have hurt the needles
and wounded the knives
extracting them
with tears of pardon
from the stones of our hearts.

We have drowned the stones
and laid on the surface
our hearts drawn on paper, –

with the evening hand we are washed
of our faultful purpose.

In a clean cup, we collect the benign
words of tongues –
                    absolved and abolished.
We leave,
  and air the room
from our wrong dust.

By the evening window, we are conceived
anew, awhite, awash with the quiet.
We forget and forgive, and sing the silence,

And sing the silence

and sing the silence

When we lie on the grass, on the snow, on the sky
and tremble for hope, for light, for sleep,
with our naked harmless arms
nailed to the means
of our being

When we hear the voice of the silence, and wait
for our names to be called
to life,
    lengthened and spelled
among the clouds,
and our naked harmless hearts
to be broken, cleansed and justified

When we see the imprints of our faces
in the grass, in the snow, – and we search in the sky,
and abandon resemblance, harmony, knowledge,
and seek the harmless, the naked,
the eyes

When we wake up and partake of the green,
the white and the blue
layers of certainty, –

and release the hold and begin to be
    and begin to be

    And begin to be.

It is the Heart's unified space,
demolished septum,
unfolded chambers, –
             that offer a home
             of an infinite enfilade.

With a muffled step,
with lowered eyes,
with your ardent lamp
             and an oil lamp,
with undone language,
disowned voice,
with the fullness of bread
          and the fullness of each crumb,

you leave the premises of your skin,
and walk down, flight by flight, up
                    your own heart's
                    stairs –
                         homewards.

And this bee and this grass fulfil their instant.

And I thirst and deny and travel

and make up for it
with a sign of the cross.

Instantwards, our hands
are dying premises. And the day is growing alive
as the hours are tolled.
Eyes winged with the weaving of nests upon belfries
count our steps in small
quantities.

And the bells are full of air
and validation,
                    and

we breathe and deny and thirst.

Song of Convalescence

As the sun replaces my eyes
with the light, with its transparent
fruit,
    I descend the sleep
and ascend the thirst.
I break the day's kernel
and sow its seeds
      from flight to flight.

As the fog replaces my skin with a white
ancient clean porcelain,
I am found
to be occupying no space,
hidden within the flowers' growth,
safe behind their scents'
curtain.

As the evening comes to replace the thirst,
to wrap my body in milk and Song,
I ascend the tune and descend the words
one by one till they melt
upon my tongue.

Winter prevails

                   we prevail with our

hopeful lowered eyelids, –

with eyes brimful of certainty,

of grey sunlight, of hours

confided to dark porcelain,

of the Advent pace of the clock. With the child's wound,

with our lake, with

our lake of the wound, –

                   baptised on

                   St. Andrew's Friday.

im Kloster

There were walls, and behind the walls.

There were quiet days, in the virtue of snow.

And time stood
outside the walls, and begged, and died for hunger.

> Its begging song clung to the bricks,
> dried out and was
> overgrown by ivy.

In the garden there were ever-fallen fruits,
ever-ripe and dwelling alone,

and the nettles were waiting
                    for a familiar hand,
to be carried in, in a basket.

By the twilit window obedience wove
its peace,
   poverty mended its riches, chastity bleached its joy,
and the woollen thread, the starch and the needle
followed the silence
of their guidance.

There were psalms at night, and soundless steps,
and the fullness of empty aisles, –
   the Presence was given without measure,
received and kept
for treasure, for bread.

The incense carried the scent of being
upwards,
   and traced the path.

There were Angels and humans, invisible to the eyes. –

   And life stood
   within the walls, and sang, and died for love.

From the 40 days of my Standing
are pressed the sap and the pulp
of my Land, –
in the motionless air I walk still,
I stand ever further towards the gate.

It is nascent and spring, before its hour
it is blossom and wound, sprouting from
                                        the earth.

Into the sky of my Land I weave
the golden thread
          of the nameless
flower.
In the field of the sky I bury my eyes,
embraces and steps, – the silent
language of my tongue.

With the dark leaves of the morning
with the birds' prayer and grey
medicine of the fog, –
                    I am landing away
beyond the indefinite kingdom
of clouds.
   On the golden tapestry of the sky
      are retraced
the face and the name
of my home.

Advental

A word whispered to a vine stalk –
at a quarter to the first hour.
barrels of water, rain's cousins,
hem the vineyard in chronological order.

A word-whisper come from the Jordan
curtails the wine's time-long way to bleeding.
A dry kneaded bread face to face with a child's beginning.
Water conveys the secret of its sanguine being.
The child dies back into the quarter past his beginning –
and is reborn
           unleavened.

Epiphany

We lay beside the cradle our weak disbelieved fears,
our wandering points, collected
and threaded
for beads of our evening telling.

We lay in the shade of the Kings' treasure
the treasure of our poverty,
of our five senses, swaddled
in the renatal cloths.

We are pasted into dry pastures,
into the sky bathed in moonlight.
Our song –
        the silence of our footfall.
We have seen. Our sight
is a star that never let us return.

We lay by the cradle the name of the snow,
the name of the ice melting to tears.
We have heard. The song of the Angels
                                is our hearing,
we become their echo and find a home.

A walk accomplished at every step
is our gold, incense and myrrh.
We have known and touched. Our walk
is a one infinite instant.

Ode to Humility

Through and throughout the fog

an upward path down the hill.
The steps that know no
                        yeast, and are
a measure
of their own
unleavened
        fullness.

The air is small and ours,
at the foot of the hill. –
                    Eyes look upwards
and are at its summit.

In the shade of the slope,
we are sheltered and safe
from our far-
  sighted walks,

            and are
            carried up
            in one another's hands.

Alms

We ask for poverty, we receive its gold,
its warm grass, its nettles and stones.

Each day gives us its day, we walk in
with a soft step, with eyes closed. We see years
                              through its curtain.

Poverty spins us a brown thread
wherewith we are hardly distinguished
from broken
forests. Its song composes our hands,
we lay them still,
they cover our knees.

From the autumn time the pavement inherits
our short walks to the chapel, a muffled footfall,
a flower laid safe in the fog.

At the porch we are mute and let subsist
on our lips
silent articulated letters.

Jn. 12:24

Sow our soil with
a sun-scourged and winnowed grain;
with the gold of your servants
tried in fire; with our binding threads
distilled and converted
into rain.

Commune once more our soil
with bread that conveys it
its pure silhouette;
give us to drink from the grain's lot
that never knew its own will.

Teach our eyes to eclipse
their reflection seen in the eyes;
extinguish the lustre of our eyelids,
the self-moon and the self-sun.

Give us an ever-barren land
yielding to our bare feet,
  yielding, for fruit, our even steps
our single hand,
our common footprints.

Transcribe
upon our palms
St. Andrew's greeting, a relic of comfort.

Deny us everything
whence
we have already been
weaned.

Let us wait, motionless,
in the middle of our pirouette –
 it is our hemisphere,
 under the cupola
 of the Earth's vapour.

The land slides off the hills.
 Let us inhabit the hill:
 with ascents, with a Calvary thought,
 with the fruits of our
 half-described circles.

Let us cut and plant the selfless tree,
the triumphant branches
 parallel to the horizon;
with our eye-sweep centred upon the crown,
with the crown, the centre of its perspective,
 reducing to vapour all other crowns.

Let us lean on the trunk – and quench
 our narrow thirst
with a sanguine infusion from its bark.
The birds of the air, denizens of the hill,
weave us a nest, as we drink –
 and with every sip
 our feathers turn white.

The just and merciful dawn shall strip us
of all the heavy load   we have spared.
Its misted gaze will lighten
to cover our naked shoulders.
       In our precious poverty
       of pearls and diamonds and living water
       drawn from wells and lachrymal glands –

we are eternally clothed.

Our cleansed leper's hands
are joined in prayer
       – and draw from the well,
         without recourse to buckets or thirst.

(Our feet, washed by the Truth's hand,
       are eternally bare, and are winged
       for the ultimate well-ward walk.)

Days of earthly exile

I wrote this sequence over a period of time where I thought I was in a complete creative sterility. It felt much like being exiled from my own element; the little I wrote also seemed alienated from where it should belong. Each of these poems came, but was reluctant to stay: I could not finish a single one, and so they remained a mass of lines jotted on bits of paper (which is the way I usually write), after a short while barely legible. Yet I felt that these apparently stillborn pieces did have life.

Having put them together, I saw that, essentially, they are one and the same poem. And that I myself, essentially, also am one and the same poem – that there is no fragmentation in them, just as there isn't any in me. And just as I myself cannot be accomplished here, in this life, so the state of being unfinished is also what is most proper to these poems. And that for those who yearn for the simple, the non-composite, the feeling of exile in this fragmented world is thus most natural.

I placed all these poems together: they neatly met, embraced – and I peacefully acquiesced to the necessity of this general (creative or existential) incompletion. I comforted myself, saying that this earthly exile would come to an end, and the single non-composite poem which I am would eventually be accomplished by its Author. That I needed to wait just a little, perhaps just a day.

1.

If we exit the circles and tune
with the linear pace of time,
and stand still and dance
and dry our flesh
around the kernel of our fruit.

                          If we fill the room
with the silent name of the sky,
once the linear course of time has folded
our hands around the clock. –

If we be and fail
to be human doings

2.

When we have outsailed the day,
        gone from our reiterated harbour,
the frail decks, elastic moorings, humid knots
left at variance with those who had never known us.

Beyond the horizon, the strings of our prayers
loosed and taut, are summoned in one accord

As a single line of a psalm   holds us above the water

3.

If we lift the anchor and furl the sail,
and walk on water
knee-deep in the sky

and wade through the clouds' reflection
in the ebb and tide of their obeisance,

the seabirds will teach us confidence,
a common faith of the chosen vessels –

transparent, unsinking, inflammable,
bearing wings for a name

4.

So we brew each day and the Hand
pours it into our clay jars.
We are emptied of birds' cries,
of wading through
                    the rain and the shine,
of counting riddles of our
retrospective foreknowledge,
of adding up knots.

We are emptied of our counter-silence,
our counter-sitting still among the clouds,
our innocent counter-riddles,
our straight (   ) lines.

5.

What is commanded is snow.
The fallen leaves' ultimate conciliation,
age bringing decay to life.
                              Dust congenial
to the lines on our fingers (they will return to it,
and tune their strings,
and learn from it
love and silence).

The leaves cling
with tears and rain. Absolved
from their dry rustle,
they nurture the earth with their
ever-renewed regrets.

With a shadowy ivy steps we weave
ourselves around the trunk

and learn to take and keep
ourselves from possessions.

6.

If the law of wisdom,
                    the law of winter –
of an empty page known
to both
eraser and pencil –
stretches its lines, furrows,
its perfect virginalised parallels,
towards the same vanishing
self-abnegating point.

If the law of perspective,
                    the law of abscission –
of a fruit living within its kernel –
elects annually its centre,

our hands will collect for a treasure
the dry leaves of the ever-clement
ever-renewed spirit of autumn

7.

There were rooms that years had filled with time,
with longing, with summer shades
thickened
to autumn shadows. – We became curtains
between the past
and the continuous endful now,
unseen and transparent, facing the front
side
of the snow, of the rain, of the shine.

We are collected with leaves and coins,
are given as alms,

are clothing the earth –

8.

As our hearing is set at rest
and our hands enfold
the riches
     of empty air

we yield to the lanterns and search
the predestined places for our steps,
dip our fingers threefold in mist
in oil and dew,
          touch the strings

and muffle the sounds.

Alone in the field, we procreate
our being with song and prayer,
we drink from the well
and learn to bear
with our failure at reading clocks

9.

That is the only world that stands, that leaves
a handful of Land
to set one's foot and deny
its very claim of being needed.

That is the only world that speaks, without
means searched and found,
through the Word it was, is, will be. –
into the ear alive through its
knowing embrace and silence.

In the midst of its meadows
the hands are filled
with water, with thirstless sunlight.

That is the world
one becomes and enters,
naked and plenty, true and a foundling.

Notes

Part 1

Land(e)scapes –

the word *Fatherland* here (and the recurrent word *Land*, further in this book) have no particular geographical reference. Since my birth I have always lived either in big cities, among stones and concrete (a narrow and stifling claustrophobic space), alternated with long stays by the sea (wide stretches of breath, of space, of being… yet not solid: melting in the horizon, liquid, escaping). A *Land* – in German this word means 'countryside' – has become for me synonymous with 'firm', 'loyal', 'selfless'; wider and more reliable than the sea, earth being deeper than waters, but with the depth that gives security; it bears no reflections, it keeps my secrets. It gives. It teaches. It receives, once the life has come to an end. It is this that I call *Fatherland*; the Land where I have learnt to say the word Father (Our Father…), the Land that immediately touches the Sky: a home, a *Heimat*.

"Silver threads of water…" –

When I was writing this poem, I couldn't quite tell from where it was coming to me, some indistinct sensations, not even images… A few hours later, I learned of the suicide of an old friend: she was a writer, had been ill for a long time and suffered, could not write any more because of the medication… In the light of the news of her suicide, the meaning of this poem became very clear to me.

Part 2

from Confessions –

The word in German is a reference to the place where this poem was written; but for the reader its 'function' here can be the following: to point at the German language, in which light the last word of this poem 'ab-solution' gains more relief, and the word 'Jubel', in the first line of the next poem, makes more sense.

Pastoral ("Via the Land...") –

The last two lines are a vague allusion to the biblical Parable of the workers of the eleventh hour.

Jn. 19:34 –

ardent lamp and an oil lamp" allude, respectively, to the Spiritual Canticle of St. John of the Cross (where he speaks of the "ardent lamp of the heart"), and to the biblical Parable of the ten virgins with their oil lamps.

Jn. 12:24 –

"St. Andrew's greeting" refers to the words of the saint before his martyrdom: "I greet you, O Cross..."

"Alms" –

The word poverty has no negative meaning, and is regarded as a virtue.

"Let us wait motionless..." –

"birds of the air" – cf. Mt. 13.31

Acknowledgements

The poems printed here have previously
appeared in the following magazines:

Envoi (nº 175, autumn 2017)
Envoi (nº 177 autumn 2018)
Envoi (nº 183, autumn 2019)
The Interpreter's House (nº 67, 2018)
Long Poem Magazine (autumn 2016)
Orbis (nº 181, spring 2018)
The Poetry Church (anthology 2018)
Poetry Salzburg Review (nº 24, 2013)
Poetry Salzburg Review (nº 30, 2017)
Poetry Salzburg Review (nº 37, 2021)
The Seventh Quarry (summer 2017)
Shearsman (nº 105, spring 2016)
Shearsman (nº 107, spring 2017)
Shearsman (nº 109, spring 2018)
Shearsman (nº 112, autumn 2019)
Snow lit rev (nº 3, spring 2015)
Snow lit rev (nº 6, spring 2018)
Tears in the Fence (nº 68, 2018)
Upstairs at Duroc (nº 17, 2018)

www.ingramcontent.com/pod-product-compliance
Lightning Source LLC
Chambersburg PA
CBHW031928080426
42734CB00007B/596